Dedication

I dedicate this book to my mom Kimberly Faison. She was always there for me through the hard times. She inspired me to write this book, I love her with all of my heart.

Introduction

This book was written to inspire all those who has ever been told they can't achieve, or ever been put down. I experienced this many times in my life especially as a teenager I was diagnosed with Asperger's Syndrome Autism. This is a disease that is supposed to limit your social skills as well as academic skills. I was told I could'nt because I was not the ideal person society thought I should be. This book was written to boost self-confidence, and to prove that with God, you can do anything if you put your mind to it. With prayer and hard work you can conquer your dreams.

Table of Contents

I Believe	02
Trace	04
I Will Endure	06
What Makes Me Stronger	08
My Broken Heart	10
Ashamed	12
Better Off Alone	14
How I Feel	16
Greed	18
Change	20
Diva	22
Innocence	24
Thankful	26
Young Single and Saved	28
God is in Everything	30
Beauty of God Inside-Out	32
It's Magic	34
My Obsession	36
My Inspiration	38

I Believe

I hope you know, I no longer feel the fear of failure, to me it's a sin. I'm determine to win, I won't let words, and your discrimination get in my way.

No longer will you dictate what I say or do.

Every day, every night I'll fight for my right.

Discriminate me you might. Unlike my pass, my future is bright.

I'm not just a pretty face; I'm driven toward winning every race.

After my dreams I will chase, nothing will stop me from reaching my destination, I have the power of determination.

I have faith in my triumphant success, in which I will achieve riches, fame, and true joy, I will receive because

"I Believe"

Trace

She's not just a pretty face, determined

    To win the race, after her dreams she will

        chase, never staying in one place after

            Her ways I wish to

                      Trace

I'll Endure

I'm going insane, the thoughts in my head I can't explain, undergoing this horrific pain.

I'm falling to the floor; I can't take this hurt anymore.

But why tell myself this, why let myself cry.

I won't let this get to me.

This is not the way it should be.

I won't allow this to kill me, I'm reaching for the light, I will never again feel as if I can't bare the suffering, I can't, no I will go on.

I'm stronger now, I believe in me at this instant, through throbbing pain through damage and hurt.

"I'll Endure"

What Makes Me Stronger

I've always had big dreams. I have the key to achieve, because in myself I believe. But do they believe in me, am I who they want me to be? I want to be known as someone magnificent, I want to make history, and I want to be a star. From where I am now, those dreams seem so far. Sitting here in the same place every day, hoping for that chance, for that opportunity to arrive. For into that sea of dreams I will dive. Hoping will get me nowhere. It takes a lot to get there, I will have to face my fears, and go through hurt, and pain. When I show them my talent they will bring me down. And tell me I'm not the most excellent, and it will give me drive. Through discourage, and fear I will survive. When I won't to break a record, they will say, I can't and won't. I say I can, and I will. In every accomplishment I will fulfill. Haters want to see me fall; they'll hate me more once they see me succeed more than them. When they underestimate me, I'll never say never. Through every obstacle through every storm, I'll hold on longer when I push myself to the limit because it's

"What Makes Me Stronger"

My Broken Heart

I fell in love with you; you fell in love with me. Deep on the inside I thought we were meant to be. You were my Romeo, I was your Juliet, everyday and night, for me you'll fight. When I felt lonely and cold you would warm me with your arms, and hold me tight. You being gone from me so long, you left me singing this sad lonely song. When I finally see you again I reach out for your love, you turn away from me, I can't believe what I see, and you taste the lips of someone else. This can't be real, because deep inside I love you still, someday you will eventually pay. Sadness, loneliness come what may, what comes up must come down; you will end up with my frown. The drama in your life will start you'll end up with

"My Broken Heart"

Ashamed

I walked into the room fear comes over me.

Afraid if they look at me what they would see in my mind, wishing fear would flee, I shake as they gag, laugh, and point at me.

And tell me I'm worthless, all because I'm not their ideal image of beauty.

Why is it that every day, I weep, every night I cry?

As if I let my faith die, I lay in bed with a pillow over my head, wishing I was dead.

Out loud I pray for fear to end, but faith, the next day in the morning I wake, I have a large goal to make. I have God on my side.

I'm beautiful, I have nothing to hide, I walk into the room, my fear has died, I'm no longer

"Ashamed"

Better Off Alone

I'm not like other wild, and narrow minded, I'm sophisticated and wide minded. I don't judge others by the color of their skin, but by the content of their character. Nor will I judge them by how they look. I'll never judge the cover of a book. What is on the outside does not determine what is within, being without a team as impossible, as it may seem. So called friends with their opinion can block me from my dream. I have no time to gossip, or judge, or lie. They come with drama of which I despise. I never had a love, I never will, because pain of a broken heart no one can heal, it's a pain I will never fill. Whenever I feel alone, when no one will answer the phone. I find Jesus is always with me, He's the light, so in the dark I can see, I'm not of this world I am a child of God. Having the power of God in me makes me stronger. I'm

"Better Off Alone"

How I Feel

I feel angry, I feel sad, and why shall I feel so bad.

Why shall I let sadness crush my joy, and take away my contentment, and peace? I got to let it go, and release.

Let happiness come over me, they are liars, while every word I speak to them inspires, I lift them up not crush them down to the ground, I love everyone around while they hate me for what I do, they make me feel so blue, why won't they believe what's true, what can help them bless others protect their brothers.

 I'm doing the will of God; he will bless me with whatever I need so gladness is

> How I feel!

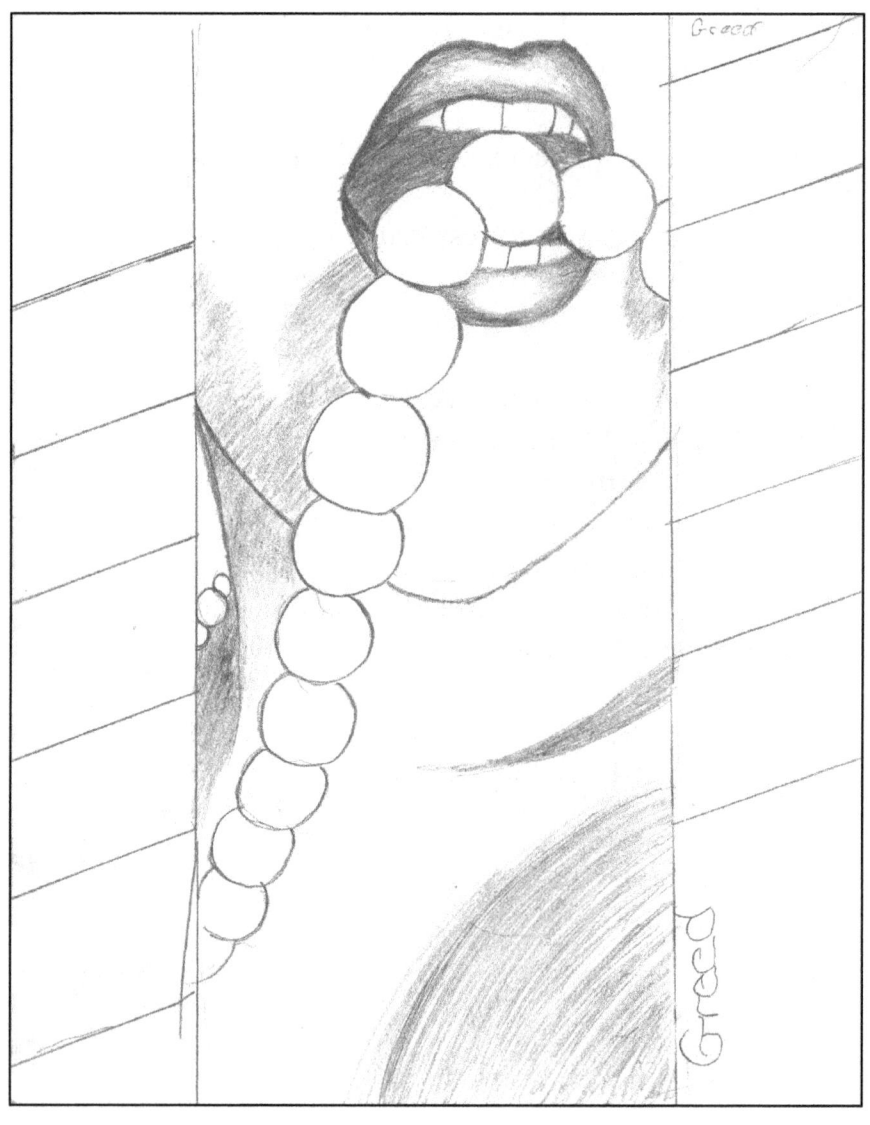

Greed

Why take, take, take, and never give, always having money is how you want to live. Why want, want, want, and never care of anyone else's feelings are you not even aware. Help a stranger do you even dare. Why steal, steal, steal and never pay. Someone might take everything from you one day; there will be nothing you can say. Why complain, complain, complain, and not be thankful because you have everything you want and more. Your house is blessed from the ceiling to the floor. Why cry, cry, cry, and never laugh because someone walks a more difficult path. Why eat, eat, eat, and never feed. Nothing can satisfy "Greed".

Change

Every morning I wake up under the same sun.

Every night I sleep under the same moon.

Every day I sit in the same chair, I write the same story while I'm sitting there.

It does not have to stay this way starting now; I will make a difference every day. Put a smile on someone's face.

Every morning I wake up with the same joy.

Every night I go to sleep with the same smile because I made a

"Change"

Diva

Her features are outstanding,
She is beautiful in every way.
She makes an accomplishment every single day,
She always finds something inspirational to say.
She stands out as a role model to every woman,
 and girl, she wants to change the world.
When it comes to winning, she's always on top,
never on bottom.
When it comes to being a hero
She is a leader not a follower; she's got big goals big dreams, and a big personality.
She's determined to make her every dream a reality.
She's a true Diva

Innocent

I was born into this world pure, I knew not this world's ways, I was unsure I knew nothing about the guilt, I would fill in the years to come.

The sorrow that would fill my head with lies.

Someday I would come to realize my sins the people I despise, when I look I see hate in their eyes, God says to love thy neighbor, as you love yourself. I speak blessings over them, and wealth, long life, and health. God wants me to praise!!! His name in his house, so I lift my hands in complete surrender to him, so my sorrow grows dim.

My guilt now fades; I look into the mirror, looking back at me, no hate in my heart, no sin in my soul.

In control I become "Innocent"

Thankful

As blessed as we are to have a place to live, money to give, we have food to eat, shoes on our feet.

Clothes on our back, Nothing in lack.

Somewhere in the world there is a child with no money, no food to eat, not even a place to sleep.

Everyday young children die.

Day and night children cry.

We should bless them with what God has blessed us with.

Make them evermore

"Thankful"

Young Single and Saved

I may be young, but I have a lot to live for.

Every day searching for an open door.

I'm a girl driven toward my dreams.

I won't let anyone stop me.

Nothing can hold me back from my success.

I will grow up to be a strong independent woman.

I'll never need a man to support me.

I can be bad all by myself.

My future is filled with wealth, I am a woman

Of God,

I'm Young Single and Saved.

God Is In Everything

I see God in the trees, I see him in the flowers, in the rushing waters of the seas.

I feel God in the air, I feel him in the breeze.

When I am tired, when I am weak, I lift my head to the sun, God's face I seek.

Then once again I am strong, at night when I am restless, I seek God's face in the moon, I seek God's face in the night sky, I feel his mercy come over me, I am content.

"God Is In Everything"

Beauty of God Inside and Out

I have a radiant glowing appearance on the Outside; I'm out going, and courageous. From the crowd I no longer hide. God shines through me, he preaches through me. I bless others with what GOD blesses me with, I'm a blessing sent from heaven, I have the "Beauty of God Inside and Out".

It's Magic

It's more than just a show; it's mastery we'll never know.

It's an indescribable experience that will leave you breathless in disbelief.

Yearning for the secret beneath.

Will anyone find the key to this dark and anonymous secrecy?

When you see it you won't believe it.

Like a never ending story, it's a happening that surpasses reality.

It's a beauty that is unseen by understanding.

It's seen by imagination, there is no explanation, can't see it with your eyes, it's what you feel with your mind, the key to which you'll never find.

It's Magic!!!

My Obsession

He's like bliss to my very eyes.

He is kind, he is humble, and extraordinarily wise.

He is like a gift, a special surprise, he is like a strong conqueror, and he is brave. I can only imagine the lives he can save, how many dreams he can pursue, because of the incredible things he can do.

How much we together could achieve, how much riches, and fame we can receive, I love him with the love of agape.

He is my friend, my hero, my love he is

"My Obsession".

My Inspiration

You are so amazing to me in time of dark you help me to see.

You told me right from wrong, wrong from right.

I hear your life giving words in a song.

For you I do no wrong.

When I was sad you gave me joy.

You lead me on the right path because of you I have the rest of my life to enjoy.

You made me who I am an amazing and wonderful person your

My Inspiration.

www.ingramcontent.com/pod-product-compliance
Lightning Source LLC
Chambersburg PA
CBHW031659040426
42453CB00006B/345